JEWELS OF JOY: MEMOIRS OF A PHYSICIAN IN TRAINING

ERICA R JONES, MD
AMANDA GRANGER, EDITOR

Dedicated Dreams
Enterprises LLC

ISBN 978-0-615-63150-9

First printing

Printed in the United States of America

Dedicated Dreams Enterprises, LLC

FOR MY FAMILY, FRIENDS, AND COLLEAGUES WHO CONTINUE TO SUPPORT MY DREAMS

Respect to my parents, Margaret Jones and Eugene Hodge for the gift of life. Special Thanks to Amanda Barnes Granger for editing, Reuel Field and Tracy Doughty for inspiration, Erika Simpson, Bridget Battles, and Traci Galbreath for their endless compassion and encouragement. Dr. Barbara Hill, my mentor, you have taught me so much. I could never show enough appreciation to my family, friends, and Sorors of Delta Sigma Theta Sorority, Incorporated for their unconditional love.

CONTENTS

INTRODUCTION

This piece of work is dedicated to my angel, the late Chasity Dione Barnes. Throughout my adult years, I have thought of several book ideas and never developed any of them. This book has been developed from my soul's outcry to Chasity; each word that you will read is comparable to several tears. As you turn each page, imagine climbing up and down a mountain of my tissue. These words are my tears. For all those who wonder, I am mourning. Share.

COURAGE

Before making one of the biggest decisions in my life, I pause, arise from the computer desk, and walk outside to my car. Some mud-covered black pumps lie on the floor behind the driver's seat. Each time I see these shoes, I get a lump in my throat, and try to ignore them. As the long, hot, summer days pass, I continue to try and ignore these dirty shoes. Some days, I would throw things on top of them. Other days, I would completely refuse to glance in that area of the car. I had decided to just throw the shoes away. Merely looking at them would bring sadness. However, today was different.

There was something special about this day. It was the day that I had to put my disdainful emotions aside and make a sound decision regarding the purchase of my first home. My mother and I had been vehemently searching for a home to purchase and move into before I started orientation for my Family Practice Residency in Huntsville. After several trips to the area, our searches resulted in no findings, and I was beginning to have second thoughts about purchasing a home altogether.

I lay in my bed and thought about how owning a home would affect my life. I grew scared as I recanted some of the first-time homeowners' horror stories that I had heard. Of my many fears, I was unsure of how I would finance any future furniture purchase and home repairs on a Resident's meager salary. I really wished I could call Chasity and get her opinion on the situation. At the age of 27, she had already purchased her first home and was making a comparable salary. A conversation with her concerning the matter would have provided great insight. Nonetheless, I was not afforded this luxury.

They say that when life gives you lemons you should make lemonade, and that's exactly what I did. I decided to stop crying and do the things that I knew Chasity would have told me. I could hear her saying, "Girl what are you scared of? God didn't put fear in the heart of man. Pray about it and then do what you gotta do to make yourself better. You see, I went ahead and bought a house once I found a job. As long as you are making sure that your salary allows you to do so, you might as well build your investments. I did it." That is what Chasity would have told me. She wasn't a fearful person; she walked in faith. Whenever she would express a doubt to me, it was soon followed by a remark concerning prayer. No matter the issue, Chasity prayed about it. She prayed about her finances, she prayed for a husband, she prayed so that she did not "have to knock somebody out," and most importantly, she prayed for everyone else—including myself.

As I gathered my thoughts, I did what Chasity and I would have agreed upon; I started praying. After I prayed, I got the courage to walk down the stairs, and outside to my car. Chasity loved shoes, and I knew that she would not have agreed with the fact that I had ruined or thrown away some beautiful pumps that I had only worn once—even if it was to her own funeral. The stride in my steps grew shorter as I approached the driver's side. It seemed that I had reached my destination all too fast, and I hesitated before I unlocked the door. I took a deep breath. Then, I opened my car door and looked at the shoes as they sat on the floor behind the driver's seat. I stared at them for a second, retrieved them, and began to wash them off with the water hose outside my mother's condominium.

The dirt was stubborn, and I reprimanded myself for waiting so long to clean the shoes off. This was no ordinary dirt; this dried red clay came from a church yard that had been soaked by heavy rains deep down in South Alabama. The dirt seemed to have formed a bond with the leather on the shoes. So, I had to drench them in water, much like I wanted to drench my face in tears as I thought about how my shoes even got this dirty.

During most of the month of March 2009, I had been celebrating "Match Day." Match Day takes place on the third Thursday of March each year. This is the day where most fourth year medical students are informed of where they have been selected to begin residency training. To be eligible to participate in the Match, students must submit money, statements, resumes, and various other documents. I found it to be a very tedious and expensive process; however, my family and friends supported me. In particular, Chasity supported me spiritually, mentally, and educationally. She was the person I called when I got frustrated. She always understood, and she always took a moment to talk-- regardless of how busy her schedule might have been. I would call her and say, "Ugh, I'm so sick of this s$%t!" Even though I knew she didn't like me to use profane language, I didn't care to control my potty mouth during the frustration. She would just say "hey hey hey! Watch the language!" and then she would proceed to tell me, "It will be worth it in the end." I listened and remained encouraged until a few days after Match Day.

A few days after matching, Chasity had informed me that the doctors in Dothan, our hometown, had performed a bone marrow biopsy and found some type of cancer that she couldn't pronounce—"something that begins with the letter A, " she had said. (I later learned the official term was adenocarcinoma of an unknown origin.) She also explained that the doctor found it hard to believe that she had cancer at such a young age, and he was puzzled about the case. Because the doctor had no options for her, she and her family decided it was best that she go to the Kirklin Clinic in Birmingham, AL. I didn't know what to think. I can recall lying in bed and texting Chasity to see how she was doing. Reading her reply to my text message shocked me. She just said, "I trust in God and him only." I really did not know how to respond to that because I had asked her how she was doing, and her response did not seem appropriate. I can't even recall how I responded, but I do remember being clueless after our text conversation.

The next day, I woke up and went to the ICU at the VA in Murfreesboro, TN to perform my duties as a fourth year medical student. I had been trained to ask the right questions to get the answers I need, but no responses from her or my family were giving me sufficient insight regarding Chasity's situation. I pondered the previous conversations and talked with my colleagues throughout the day. There was still no valid answer to my questions. As a fourth year medical student, getting second-hand information was very frustrating. I did not have enough experience to know exactly what she was talking about, but I did know that the prognosis was not good if cancer was found in the bone marrow. I wanted more answers, but I did not want to aggravate the situation by asking several questions. The family was upset already, and Chasity did not seem to be able to give me any more information.

Chasity could not provide more insight into her medical condition at the time, but she definitely gave me insight for the future. She showed courage that I have never seen before. She knew that she had a life-threatening ailment, and it didn't affect her character or how she treated others. I know that she was saddened about the situation, but she never allowed her weakness to show--her faith in God did not waiver. She was willing and ready to face anything with her God. In one of our conversations, she told me, "I don't know what is going on, but the devil is a liar and I will not let him steal my joy." I know that she realized that her health was deteriorating. Nevertheless, she would not allow anything, even the thought of death, to take her happiness.

Chasity was great in this way. She recognized an obstacle, stared it down, and dared it to get in her way--COURAGE. This courage is now engrained in my spirit. I know that I have not been given the spirit of fear. Therefore, I will be strong when faced with obstacles. I asked myself the following questions: Will you be able to recognize and overcome your obstacles like Chasity did when faced with the reality of her imminent death? Will you face your problems or run from them?

FAITH

After spending an evening with some of my soon-to-be departing friends, I received a phone call. My mother advised me to go to Birmingham because Chasity was being admitted to the hospital there. This was shocking because Chasity didn't sound really sick over the phone. We had been talking and texting as usual. Although she was sick, I realized that all I could do was to continue to communicate and not treat her any different. I was hundreds of miles away, so all I could do was call and text. Throughout our interaction, she remained positive and her voice never trembled. She asked me how school was going, and we talked about our upcoming London trip.

Neither Chasity nor I had ever been out of the country. So, we decided back in December that we would go on an adventure. We asked other friends and family to join us, but no one else was interested or had the finances. We agreed to take the trip without the rest; just the two of us would explore the world. We called each other one night and booked our tickets for seats on two nearby rows. This way we could both have views from window seats. We were adventurous and looked forward to seeing many of the sites. We had planned to go shopping, to cross the London Bridge, to witness the changing of the guards at Buckingham Palace, and to ride the Double Decker buses on a tour of the city. A long-time friend of the family was going to host us throughout our stay; we were excited. The conversation with my mother helped me to realize that these plans were going to be postponed. I gathered some of my belongings, placed them into a suitcase, left Nashville, and headed to Birmingham.

Aunt Bet (Chasity's mother) asked me to bring her a chicken box to the hospital while I informed her that I was on the way. I found a Wal-Mart after arriving to Birmingham; I went in and bought Chasity a couple of stuffed animals to cheer her up. Easter was approaching, so I got a singing bunny rabbit. I hurried to my car because I knew that my aunt had been waiting for me to bring her food. I drove around for an extra thirty minutes without finding a nearby chicken restaurant. So, I went ahead to the hospital room to find out if she had any other food preferences. Chasity was sitting up in bed when I entered the room. I hugged her and gave her the singing bunny. She enjoyed the song it sang. She smiled. Shortly after, we took a walk around the hallways near her room. We laughed and joked about something the nurses and doctors were doing and headed back to the room. I noticed that she was weak, and her hair was a bit frazzled. It was very unlike Chasity to have one hair out of place. Her makeup was always flawless, garments were lightly pressed, and her fragrance would enlighten a room. She was taller than me, standing approximately 5'6" with wide hips. Her fair skin, which was usually glowing from the kiss of the Destin sun, was pale. Her hair was a bit withered. She hadn't lost much weight, but she seemed frail to me.

She was obviously in pain. As she rested from our walk, Aunt Bet sat on the side of her bed and rubbed her back. Chasity was not very talkative, but I knew that she was enjoying my company. We chatted for a little while, and I left to go get some food for myself and my aunt. I walked around the vicinity of the hospital and found a McAllister's closeby. The closest she was going to get to a chicken box was a grilled chicken breast. I got that for her, something for myself, and some Cheetos for Chasity. Cheetos were Chasity's favorite chips. When I got back, she was resting in her hospital bed. Her mom and I ate our food while she slept.

I had brought my laptop along on the trip, and I used it to play some of Chasity's favorite gospel songs. She really enjoyed listening to the music, and even sang along to most of the songs. When she wasn't singing Aunt Bet would take over. I sat on the side of the bed half of the time. I could tell that the music had lifted her spirits. Chasity began to sit up and talk more. We laughed about the London trip. She said, "Erica I don't think we're going to make it to London this time." I replied, "Girl I dunno! We just might! Who knows?" I truly believe that hope is uplifting--even when one knows that his or her fate is dismal.

While we were talking I was observing Aunt Bet; she was exhausted, but refused to leave Chasity's side for anything--even to go to the snack machine. As the gospel music played in the background, the mother and daughter pair quoted scriptures back and forth. I had never seen such a thing before. Chasity would say things like, "I trust in God and I believe that he will do his will."

A few hours after we ate dinner, Chasity had an alarming episode. We were all sitting down listening to the music, and she sat up in bed and clenched her chest. She said, "I can't breathe!! My chest is burning!! Jesus help me!" I ran to the bedside and witnessed her gasping for air as her eyes began to roll to the back of her head. I began to scream her name, "Chasity, Chasity!!!" Her eyes reopened and the moment she caught her breath, she said, "Satan I rebuke you."

This was a powerful moment.

In the midst of trouble, Chasity believed that the Lord was going to rescue her. She called on Jesus' name in her time of need, which is what we are taught to do as Christians. It was amazing to me that she would have the mindset to call on his name as soon as she could breathe. Her first sound was Jesus. It made me wonder how much trouble I could have avoided in my life by staying focused on Jesus. At this point, Chasity definitely used Jesus to escape her pain. She wasn't worried about the fact that she couldn't breathe for several seconds. Her only concern was trying to withstand her attack from the devil and focusing on her Lord.

This moment was almost surreal. As she panted for air, her mother just began to pray and quote scriptures. It was as if they had escaped reality and entered into a new realm. I watched them like a movie. Aunt Bet paced from side to side of the room singing and Chasity finally lay down. I saw her mother take a sigh of relief. I thought to myself, "Chasity is not looking good." In retrospect; she was likely suffering from a massive blood clot.

Shortly after Chasity had the shortness of breath, the nurse came in and drew blood for lab work. Several doctors came in to reveal the results. Then, I thought to myself, "This is not good." When her treatment team entered the room I could tell that the message they had to relay was not a positive one. The blank stares that covered their faces said it all. I too have had to wear the mask of the stoic--it covers the tears that come from your heart and the fear that your brain produces. I quickly recognized this mask. Therefore, I braced myself.

A tall, dark-haired, fair skinned male stepped in front of the group and said, "We got your results back, and you seem to be in DIC." He began to explain the meaning of DIC-Disseminated Intravascular Coagulation, and I stopped listening. My thoughts had been reaffirmed. I knew that this meant that she would likely not recover from her illness. This was the end. The conversation faded back in as he asked Chasity if she understood, and she repeated everything back to him word for word.

I'm not sure what the physicians discussed after they left, but Chasity received a phone call from a female physician minutes later. She said that she was calling to make sure that Chasity fully understood what was going on. Moments later she handed me the phone, and I introduced myself as a 4th year medical student. She explained to me that my cousin was in critical condition, and she would likely be transferred to the ICU. We discussed possibly starting blood thinners at this point, and she emphasized the importance of informing everyone of the critical nature of Chasity's health. After hanging up the phone Chasity explained to me that she knew what was going on, and we called the rest of the family.

As she sat in the chair to the right of Chasity's bed, Aunt Bet said, "Erica I'm glad you came. I'm tired." Shortly after, she was sound asleep in the chair. I was happy that she took a few moments to rest. I'm sure she had not been sleeping much over the past couple of days. Time passed as my cousin and I talked about old times and all the fun that we had. My laptop served as a great form of entertainment. We looked at old pictures from different events that we had attended. We reminisced on one concert in particular. LL Cool J, an older rapper, was scheduled to perform; Candance (Chasity's youngest sister), Chasity, and I were excited to see this beautiful man!! The concert was being held at the Dothan fairgrounds, and the ground was still soft from rain on the previous day. LL Cool J was so fine and sexy. We couldn't wait to see him. The announcer began to introduce him, and we ran towards the stage. Suddenly I saw Chasity disappear from my peripheral and reappear as she slid through the mud!! She had slipped on a soft spot in the soil and ruined her pants!! Instead of being sad or crying, Chasity immediately got up. She told Candance and me, "you all stay right here and I am going to change." Mesmerized by LL Cool J, Candance and I stood there and watched. Before we knew it, Chasity had returned with no negative feelings. Those were good times. I told Chasity, "You were just a little bit too happy about LL. So happy you bust your butt!!" She laughed.

We went through most of the pictures that were on my laptop that night. Gospel music from my iTunes program played in the background. We laughed and talked about other events that we had attended as well. When she grew sleepy I moved from her bedside to the let out bed in the corner of her room. I lay on that bed for hours and could not sleep. Fortunately, I had a friend that liked to stay up late at night to keep me somewhat distracted. I watched Chasity sleep the entire time, and she seemed so peaceful. I only remembered her waking up once to say that she was hot, and I got her a cold, wet towel to put across her head. Aunt Bet was sound asleep, snoring loudly in the chair on Chasity's right side. My friend and I text each other throughout the night and talked about random topics until I fell asleep. I am grateful for the time my friend spent with me over the phone, and I am even more appreciative of the happy times I got to share with Chasity.

Have you ever thought about what the topic of conversation would be if your loved one was on his or her death bed? Have you ever thought about things that you would share with the world as you left?

Chasity made me think about all these things. She shared so much with me in her final hours. She demonstrated never-ending FAITH. What will you show the world in your final hours? Will people remember what you believed in?

STRENGTH

I must have been sleeping deeply because I felt that I was rudely awakened by a stranger's voice. I cracked my eyes open enough to see a thin, brown skinned man speaking to my family. I don't remember much of the conversation, but I remember feeling a somnolence engulf the room. Shortly after the doctor left, more family members arrived. I felt comfort in knowing that others had come to join us on this journey. Smiles and sorrow surrounded Chasity, Aunt Bet, and I while we entertained guests. During the evening hours, our path changed direction.

This journey was one that began unexpectedly, and we were not prepared. The most preparation that had been taken was the act of packing our things and getting them in order so that we could leave Chasity's hospital room. The medical team had informed us that she was being transferred to a room in CCU. They told us that they were going to place a central line for better IV access once she got into The Unit. With that being said, I knew that Chasity's health was quickly deteriorating.

Chasity was the type of woman that wanted to be well informed and in full control; at this critical point, she looked to me for answers. I explained to her that they were going to put an IV in her neck so that they could get better access to her major arteries and veins. I also told her that it was going to hurt a little bit, but not to worry. I gave her two thumbs up and she gave me one back as they wheeled her from the room. In her last moments, she never cried. I paused, looked around the big empty room, and the reality of the situation continued to set in. All of our things had been sitting in this one corner of the room, and now it seemed empty as Kitty (Chasity's oldest sister), Aunt Bet, and I stood there. Kitty said, "We can just get this stuff together so we can move it to another room when Chasity's gets back from ICU. All the while, I knew that she probably would never return from the ICU. Reality had set in for me. Through my medical education, God had given me foresight. I knew that it was my duty to lead my family through this tough time.

We carted our personal items from the hospital room to the ICU waiting room. It was fairly desolate. I chose some chairs towards the back of the room for Bet, Kitty, and I to rest in. It had been a long day. Kitty had arrived in town from Savannah that same day; Aunt Bet had slept in the chair overnight; and I had stayed up all night with Chasity after driving in from Nashville the prior night. We each chose a pair of chairs and secured our belongings alongside us. Kitty and Aunt Bet settled in. I was tired, but nowhere near sleepy.

Luckily, I brought a book along. I had been reading a workbook to prepare for my ACLS certification exam that I would be taking once I started residency. There were a few different logarithms that I wanted to learn very well so I would be prepared to lead code teams in the hospital. I was interrupted only after a short while of reading by a strange occurrence. A small boy walked up to me and started to converse.

I thought this was strange because there was no adult in the surrounding area. This little boy was walking around the waiting room after midnight without shoes. He asked me, "What are you doing?" I replied, "Oh nothing just a little reading." He proceeded to hold small talk for a few minutes and I asked him, "What are you doing here?" He replied, "Oh I'm just waiting on the rest of my friends." I was shocked by his reply because there was no one else in the waiting room. I looked at my cousin Amanda and laughed. I couldn't take this kid serious! I wanted to make sure I wasn't hallucinating. She looked at the little boy and smiled.

During our conversation, I allowed him to play with my book and draw on some white paper. While he doodled on the arm of my chair I kept wondering why no one had come to look for their child. He doodled his name, "Vincent" in what seemed to be a 5-year-old's handwriting. Then, just as quick as he skipped up to me, he was ready to depart. He said well, I have to go now; I have to go meet up with the rest of my friends. Then he ran off. I was still confused, and I was growing tired. Aunt Bet and Kitty were dozing in and out of sleep.

I couldn't stop wondering what was taking the doctors so long to place the central line. At least an hour had passed, and we hadn't received any notification of Chasity's status. I walked over to the phone, slowly picked it up, and asked the nurse if the family could come back and visit. She informed me that we would be notified when Chasity was stable. I thanked her and hung up the phone. I went back to the area where my family was sitting and notified them. Soon after, they fell asleep.

After speaking with and texting a close friend, I grew

drowsy. Then, I heard an announcement, "Code Zero in CCU Bed 22." The thunder of doors slamming and the patter of quickly moving feet flooded the barren hallways. My heart dropped. I knew that the description of the location was probably Chasity's bed. Kitty asked me, "Is that Chasity's bed they are calling over the intercom?" I didn't say a word. All I could do was give her a blank stare. I just looked at her!! I felt Chasity's departure in my soul. It was almost as if someone had ripped a piece of my heart away without invading my body cavity. There was nothing I could do. So, I sat there and waited. I was unsure of how the next moments would unfold, but I was sure of what had happened. I knew that my cousin was gone and she was the friend that Vincent was waiting on. He had to have been an angel.

After what seemed like hours, a guy in scrubs came out and said, "Barnes Family." It seemed as though I had already lived through this once because I had a sense of peace. Aunt Bet and Kitty followed him through a set of doors to another part of the hospital. I sat and waited. They emerged from the ICU doors a few minutes later, and I could tell that the news wasn't good. Kitty said, "She's gone." I don't remember saying anything. I just remember hugging her, and then my aunt.

Shortly thereafter, a chaplain came out to escort us to the bed where Chasity's body was lying. He gave us his condolences and offered to bring some chairs into the ICU room. We refused the chairs and stood at the bedside. Still, my tears did not form. I stood there for about 45 seconds and looked at the body that once held my cousin's spirit, and then I looked away. Her sister and her mother were very upset, and I knew that it was my job to help comfort them.

I made a valiant effort at being strong that night. As we left the room, Kitty looked at me and said, "You knew already didn't you?" I kept quiet and gave her a hug. We walked back to the small room where the chaplain met us again. He gave us his card, and instructed us to inform him of the name of the funeral home that was going to be responsible for the ceremony. He left the room, and the three of us sat there. We sat there in an unfamiliar room contemplating. Important decisions had to be made, although our souls cried out. We had to call home and tell someone what had happened. This situation proposed some interesting questions. I think everyone should seriously consider the answers to the following questions.

Who is the first person you would call to tell such news? Which of your friends or family would be strong enough to support you in your time of need? Who would answer your phone call at 3am?

Aunt Bet, Kitty, and I had to ask ourselves these questions while under duress. After making a few phone calls we were able to inform our family. Then a funeral home had to be chosen. I was amazed at the strength of my aunt. She made these decisions in seconds, and without having an acute psychiatric episode. Once these decisions were made, we went into autopilot. We loaded our belongings from a hospital cart into my small sports car. The trunk was already full of several bags that I had packed in case of a long stay in Alabama. We managed to fit all of our things into my car and we began our journey to Dothan.

We drove through a smothering blanket of darkness. With each mile, I felt as though I would lose my breath. It was hard to even begin to process the fact that my cousin had died. So, I stopped thinking about what had happened. I put in a gospel cd and cleared my mind. I focused on the yellow reflectors in the middle of the road. Outside of the occasional street light, taillights and headlights, they seemed to be the only source of constant luminescence. We grew closer to bigger cities, and my longing for the end of this journey grew stronger. There was no giving up. I had to finish the course. I had to make sure my family was alright and get them there safely. I wanted to speed, but I knew that wasn't smart. So, I placed the car in cruise control when I could, and drove on. At some point, night turned to day and we eventually made it into Webb, AL.

Everything seemed to happen in slow motion as I turned onto the road on which Aunt Bet lived. From a distance, I could see cars covering the land in front of the Barnes family home. I drove closer and my brain began to interpret spots against a background as several people. The first person I picked from the crowd was my grandmother. I pulled into the yard, parked the car, and got out. I don't remember looking at Bet or Kitty.

I walked into the yard and hugged various family members; my grandmother was the last person that I embraced. Feeling my grandmother's arms wrapped around me comforted my spirit. I felt like an infant who had just been fed and swaddled in a fresh warm blanket. I had no care in the world at that moment. In her arms, I was transformed into a baby--I did not have to be strong anymore. I wept for several minutes as she held me. I believe that moment was my weakest to date.

Our family provided support as strong as the foundations of the pyramids of Giza. They helped with the arrangements and everything else that was needed to honor Chasity's memory. With that being said, I thought that the most difficult part of the journey was over. The only duty left was to attend the funeral services. In my short lifetime, I have learned that it is necessary to have a support system to lean on. Who do you lean on? Do you utilize your support system or attempt to serve as your own?

JOY

Upon our arrival, the church parking lot was reaching capacity. I knew it would be like this because people loved Chasity; she was a local celebrity. My favorite cousin had appeared on billboards and the cover of schedule booklets for Troy University. People would often stop her and say, "Hey you're that girl on the billboard," and she would say "yep that's me!" She embraced the popularity she had gained, and always said, "I'm going to be a star. You just watch and see." Chasity had also been responsible for marketing at the Southeast Alabama Medical Center. Her boss Rick Smith could attest to Chasity's dream to be a star, and he was always there to support her aspirations.

Chasity valued Rick's position in her life. She cherished the faith he had in her abilities and admired his leadership capacity. I can remember her saying, "My boss is a little young, light-skinned guy with braces. He's cute too! But he has a wife and kids and you know I'm not interested in that. God is gonna send my husband soon though. I've been praying." As a single, twenty-five year old popular medical student, I could not understand for the life of me why she wanted to get married! I was enjoying the single life. Chasity and I were so different, but we understood one another very well. Her most important goal was to discover the husband that God made for her and to build a family with this man.

There was nothing about her that a person could form negative thoughts about. Chasity was a beacon of joy. No matter where she was, she was making a valiant attempt to create some type of joy. She was the giddy one amongst her friends, the socialite amongst her sisters, and the happy public relations girl at work. There were few days when you would see Chasity without a smile on her face, and I keep that smile close to my heart. When I reflect on the past, it is this smile that helps me through the tough times.

It was a rainy afternoon in March when we sat through a memorial service, better known as a funeral, for an hour or so and listened to her friends speak about her life. The choir sang intermittently, and our pastor of over ten years delivered the eulogy. I was amazed that he could ascend into the pulpit without shedding one tear. Reverend Wayne Lampley is a great pastor. He led a very small congregation at the Sardis Missionary Baptist Church. It was that very same churchyard that held the stubborn red clay that was stuck to my shoes. He builds great relationships with the members and knows each of our names, but I always found it amazing how he managed to call Candance by Chasity's name every Sunday when he acknowledged her duty as an Usher. It almost seemed as if it was some sort of joke that he told to end the monotonous rituals of our old Southern Baptist Church service. After he gave the sermon and invited the congregation to discipleship, he would thank the ushers standing at the door of the Lord's house; usually these were the same dedicated people every week. He would say, "I would like to thank Mother Jones," (my 80 year old grandmother), and sister Chasity—I mean Candance for standing at the doors of the church."

Although this was no regular church service, I definitely needed some type of uplift; I needed him to say something profound—something that would mend my heart. I had no idea what he was going to speak about because Chasity had changed her membership to another church, and had not been around Sardis much in the past several months. The church quieted, and he began to speak about making a joyful noise. He said that Chasity made a joyful noise unto the Lord, and that made my heart smile. He supported this statement with examples from her life.

Chasity was a musician. I cannot recall how old she was when she began to play the piano, but I can remember how good she was. She could read music, and play it exceptionally well. Chasity and I had both taken piano lessons as children, but I quit in an act of defiance. I refused to clip my fingernails. I was a strong-willed soul even in my younger years, and something about this old lady demanding that I cut my fingernails off didn't sit well with me. So, I quit. Chasity told me that I was silly for that, and she continued to play. This talent thrust her into the forefront of the church community. She was known as one of the best skilled pianists around town.

Chasity was a witness. I enjoy the music and social experience that some night clubs have to offer. One night Chasity and Candance went along with me during a weekend they were visiting me in Nashville. I took them to what was then called Level 88 Jazz Bistro and Bar. The setting provided sultry jazz that seduced the ear, and a sophisticated crowd that was unconcerned about the novelties of the nightlife; tired from the stress of working throughout the week, the patrons just wanted to have a goodtime. I knew I could bring Chasity here for a night of fun. She doesn't drink alcohol or do much dancing, but she enjoyed the nightlife as well. She was a social butterfly. I can remember leaving to go get a drink and coming back to find Chasity engaged in a deep conversation with this really handsome guy. I assumed that he was attempting to get her number, and she was enjoying the conversation. Because she seemed so engaged, I decided not to disturb her.

The musicians played the most tantalizing rhythms and my alcohol marinated my body. After thirty minutes, I looked over and Chasity was still talking to this guy. I had to go see what was going on! I approached the two, and as I got closer I could hear Chasity say something about Jesus. I said girl, "What are yall over here doing?" She said, "honey we over here talking 'bout the Lord."
I laughed at the thought of these two people in the club talking about the Lord. Chasity soon finished her conversation and headed back over to talk with me and Candance. I had a couple more drinks and we headed out. Thoughts about Chasity's boldness continued to arise. It amazed me how this girl just didn't care where she was. She was not afraid to tell people how good God had been to her.

Chasity was a family woman. Earlier, I spoke about her desire to start a family. I admired Chasity because she did not rush into a relationship; she would always say, "I'm gonna pray about this guy and see if this is who God has sent me." Several of our family members had children out of wedlock, and she refused to repeat history. Family was vital to Chasity. She loved entertaining her nieces and nephews, and rarely missed a family event. She supported each of us in our accomplishments. I can remember her saying, "When is your graduation? Girl, I need to make sure that I'm off right now. You know I wouldn't miss it for the world." I keep this statement close to my heart because it reminds me that Chasity had to leave us to serve a higher purpose. Nothing in the world would have kept her from missing my graduation from medical school. So she must be doing some celestial work. No matter what she is doing, I can guarantee that Chasity Dione Barnes is making a joyful noise.

What type of noise have you made? What impact would you like to leave on the world?

INTELLIGENCE

Despite my ability to function at a high intellectual level, I could not process Chasity's death. The synapses did not fire. The rain skewed my vision as I attempted to peer out of the window from the limo to the gravesite. There were several people who had reached Sardis before the family limo in which I was riding had arrived. I had taken countless numbers of trips to Sardis throughout my life, yet this one seemed unreal. This trip to Sardis seemed so unfamiliar. Sheets of rain continued to fall. I stepped out into the mud in disbelief. My mother comforted me. It was difficult to process the fact that my big cousin, who was like a sister to me, was no longer alive. My mother and I walked to the gravesite together. As my heels sank into the red clay, my heart sank further and further into my chest. The casket had been closed and roses were being passed out. I took one and held it as I listened to Rev. Lampley say his final goodbyes. After the final prayer, the loved ones threw the roses into the gravesite and we walked away. I don't remember much after that--not even the ride back home.

It was hard to accept that one of my favorite people would no longer be in my life. I adored Chasity. My admiration of her began over 10 years ago when she used to show me the Honor Roll plaques that she would receive every year from Webb Junior High School. I would wonder why Dothan City Schools didn't give us plaques, because I wanted to be like my big cousin. This admiration grew as we did. She went off to college at Troy State University while I was still in high school in Roswell, GA. I knew that I wanted to be a doctor, but had no idea where I wanted to attend college. I had been receiving letters from schools all over the country, and because of the high score that I made on the ACT; I knew that I would probably get scholarships to all of these places. After discussing the issue with my mom, I decided to attend Florida A&M University's School of Business and Industry. They had offered me the most scholarship money, and one of my close friends was also planning to attend school there as well. Yes, I know those are all the wrong reasons! Needless to say, I was looking for another University to transfer to by mid-September. Chasity always seemed happy with her current situation, and she had told me nothing but good things about the university she attended. She was majoring in Broadcasting/Journalism and loved it. Before I knew it, I was joining Chasity at Troy State University.

Soon after I joined her at TSU, Chasity graduated with a Bachelor's Degree in Public Relations. She began a successful career, and I graduated and went to medical school. A few years after entering the workforce, Chasity was smart enough to realize that her earning power would be multiplied by earning a Master's Degree. Not only did she enroll in a Master's Program, but she also encouraged a close friend and her youngest sister to join her as well. Intelligence combined with the ability to motivate others results in an extraordinary person. I saw her as such. Chasity excelled in everything that she did. She was not satisfied with mediocracy, and had big goals. Because she was so goal-oriented and focused on success, she had her affairs in order. Chasity was intelligent enough to realize that she could work and continue to do the things she loved, which included playing the piano for local churches and traveling. She managed her time effectively by balancing work and personal time.

One of the smartest things that she used to do was setting aside what she called, "ME TIME." Every so often, Chasity would drive down to Destin, Florida alone. Sometimes we would talk while she was on her way there or back home. She would tell me how she just needed to spend some time with herself and her God. She would say, "girl I needed a break! I was so stressed out, and I knew that I just had to get away." She would tell me how much she enjoyed laying on the beach in prayer and meditation. Chasity was smart enough to make time for her spiritual needs. I now know that this is one of the most intelligent things that a person can do.

Have you been smart enough to take time to reflect on the person you have become and the person you would like to be? Can you recognize when you are at a point in your life that requires a de-stressor?

LOVE

My shiny black, washed off pumps sat on the bathroom floor of my mother's condominium, and I wanted to throw them away. I'm sure that most females would probably think that I was crazy for having that urge, but it was genuine. It didn't seem to matter that I had only worn the shoes once. What mattered to me at the time were the memories they represent; I didn't want to think about it that day. It hurt too much. It hurts too much. It hurts a lot. I think it will always hurt. However, I know that I must deal with the pain.

So I decided to keep these shoes, for my mental health. My conscious would not let me throw them away. After all, throwing them away wouldn't alleviate the pain the memories held. I could hear Chasity say, "Girl I know you are not throwing away those nice heels for no good reason!" She loved shoes, and preferred heels!! She was a DIVA! Even while playing the piano for hours at church she would bang on those keys and pedals in two inch heels —making sure that she looked good the entire time. Not only did she make sure she looked good, but she also put forth a lot of effort into ensuring that the people she loved looked good. I remember a conversation we had about appearance several years ago. She emphasized the importance of looking good because it demonstrated how much you care about yourself. Chasity loved herself and it showed daily.

Outside of looking good, Chasity had a strong desire to help our youth. She loved children. At least one time each month for a few months, Chasity would hold sleepovers at her house for the youth of the church at Sardis. During these sleep-overs, Chasity would teach the children skills with money management and social interaction. She would take them to the movies, mall, and even to the local fair. Her love for mankind--especially children, was immeasurable.

What do you love to do? Have other people witnessed you declare and express your love?

PEACE

Success had always been a heavy topic of conversation between Chasity and I. I can recall driving around Nashville one night as I was speaking to her on the phone. She was telling me about how she had just left Bible study, and how she learned so much. I asked her what she learned, and she began to tell me a story about how God has selected specific angels to protect us during our time here on earth. She told me about Gabriel, the archangel, who had appeared to Daniel and was a messenger for God. She told me that there were different kinds of angels that were all here to support God's children. Soon after she finished that sentence, the conversation was interrupted by a phone call from her boyfriend. No matter how short that conversation was, it was priceless. The depth of its content sticks with me up until this very moment. Reflecting on that conversation gives me a sense of peace. It seems to have been some type of foreshadowing—a type of connection that her spirit made with mine—to prepare me for the hard times to come. In retrospect, she was giving me peace and letting me know that everything would be alright. She was reassuring me that I would not be left alone.

Oftentimes, a person's death leaves the family in emotional, spiritual, and financial disarray. However, Chasity's passing was quite different. She was intelligent enough to have her business in order. As the old folks at Sardis Missionary Baptist Church sing in their hymnals, Chasity had her "house in order." Not only had she given her life to Christ, but she also insured her life. Life insurance is something that most people in their twenties don't think about. We oftentimes get caught up in "trying to get a job and paying off student loans" that we forget to insure ourselves. If my job did not offer a certain amount of life insurance, I'm not sure if I would have thought about attaining it. Chasity thought about all these things. She left her business affairs in order so that her family did not have to struggle to close several accounts and pay large amounts to debtors. She was always good about paying anything that she owed. Because Chasity did not believe in having children out of wedlock, she did not leave any children behind. Chasity Dione Barnes left us in peace with a legacy that will never die. She was my cousin and my sister; I could never forget what she believed in.

When you are no longer able to provide--either in life or death, what will you leave your family with? Do you have your affairs in order? Will your family be left with difficult decisions that you could have made?

Although we were not blood sisters, Chasity and I had such a strong relationship that an outsider could not tell. As a matter of fact, we were kids and Aunt Bet would take me to the mall with Candance and Chasity, people always thought that I was her child. We all used to wear the same matching outfits; they would only vary in color. Chasity was the oldest, and she would always boss me and Candance around. Most of the time we didn't mind too much. It makes me chuckle to think about how Chasity always wanted to be in charge. It didn't matter if we were making mud pies or cleaning up; Chasity was going to tell everybody what to do and how to do it. That's what I call a natural born leader!

I love my cousin dearly and miss her more than I could ever express. Sometimes I find myself scrolling through the C's in my phonebook to look for her number--only to be reminded that she will never answer again. It's a constant disappointment—a let-down that will be followed by so many more in life. Nevertheless, it gives me peace to know that Chasity remains a leader, in life and death. Her spirit is in me, and so many more that she touched. Chasity often said, "I am going to be a superstar!" I must say this to my cousin, "Babe, you were right once again. You are a superstar. Your energy continues to touch others' lives, just as the sun simultaneously kisses the honey dew drops on a million rose petals. I love you and miss you dearly.

EPILOGUE

My younger sister Chasity was always a headstrong, determined person. Even when she was a little girl, she would go after anything she wanted – no matter what anyone had to say. For example, there was an incident that occurred while I was babysitting my three younger sisters. She couldn't have been any more than 10 at the time. Chasity wanted a corndog from the country store, which was at least a mile or so away from our home. I told her that I could not take her to the store. It was probably because she didn't need the corndog anyway. In genuine fashion, she hopped on her bike and left. I was terrified. My first stop in the search for Chasity in the tiny town of Webb, Ala. was obviously the little store that sold the corndogs. That is where I found her, corndog and all. She didn't care about the consequences or repercussions she would face when our parents found out. She was determined to get what she wanted. And she always did.

She was determined to be class valedictorian of her junior high class. And she was. She was determined to get a scholarship and go to college and she did. She was determined to get a job in her field of public relations and she did. She wanted an M.B.A. and she got it. At the age of about 25 she wanted to be public relations director at hospital and she did. She wanted to own her own home and car. And she did. See the pattern? What Chasity wanted, Chasity got.

Chasity knew that she did nothing on her own. Everything was through the will of God. She loved God with everything that was in her. She wasn't afraid to let anyone know either. Jesus was the head of her life and you didn't even have to ask. She exuded him. She glorified him. She praised him. She gave thanks all the time. She was a strong follower.

In her last days, she held on to that faith that she had carried with her. She was willing to accept God's will for her life – although it might not have been what she wanted or expected. Like the old church folk used to say, she was a soldier in the army of the Lord. When the enemy took over her body in the form of cancer and blood clots, she held on to the words of God and his promises to her.

I know that she never imagined that at 27-years-old that she would be getting ready to see her Lord and Savior face-to-face. But she was ready. If anyone was ready, she was ready. She told me so just hours before her appointment with Jesus.

She sat up in her hospital bed and said, "I'm not worried about me or my soul." I told her that there was no reason why she should have been. In my heart I knew that God wanted the best for himself. Chasity had a larger job to handle in God's Kingdom. We realized that she had done all she could here on earth.

A couple of days after she went to be with her Lord, I was going through some of her things. I picked up one of her memory books from high school. There was a spot in there for her to list the person she most admired. To my surprise, she had written my name there. I never knew that Chasity followed my actions so attentively. I've learned that you must always be aware of the lives you can potentially influence. Chasity did not know that she is one of the people that I admired the most. Her determination and faithfulness to God is something that I strive for daily.

We are all put on this earth for a reason. Live up to God's expectation of you. I can speak for myself when I say that I will. Why? Not only do I want my name to be in the Book of Life when I get to the gates of Heaven, but I can't wait until the day I can see my sister's precious face again.

-Amanda Barnes Granger

Chasity smiling on Troy University's main campus

ORDER FORM

Quantity	ISBN	Title	Release Date	Price

MAIL TO:

Dedicated Dreams Enterprises
210 Shadowbrook Lane
Huntsville, AL 35811

Date:
Phone:
E-Mail:

Ship to:
Address:
City & State:
Zip Code:

Total for books:
Shipping charges (add: $4.95 per book):
Total Enclosed:

Sorry for the inconvenience but we do not accept personal checks. Money orders and certified bank checks only please.